Saint Ignatius of Loyola

A Convert's Story

Patrick Corkery SJ

First published in 2021 by Messenger Publications

ISBN: 9781788123273

All excerpts from the Autobiography are taken from Joseph Tylenda's
A Pilgrim's Journey: The Autobiography of St. Ignatius of Loyola
(San Francisco: Ignatius Press, 2001). Used with permission.

Designed by Messenger Publications Design Department
Typeset in Adobe Garamond Pro and Administer
Printed by W & G Baird

Messenger Publications,
37 Leeson Place, Dublin D02 E5V0, Ireland
www.messenger.ie

Dedication

This book is dedicated to my late mother, who taught me to read. It is one of the most important gifts I've ever been given.

Acknowledgements

My thanks to Donal Neary SJ, who invited me to write this booklet. I am fortunate with where I work and with my Jesuit community, so I am grateful to Damon McCaul, headmaster of Gonzaga College and Richard O'Dwyer SJ, superior of Gardiner Street Jesuit Community. I'm thankful to several Jesuits who looked at parts of this book while being written and gave me encouragement and feedback. My thanks to Patrick Carberry SJ, Niall Leahy SJ, Dermot Mansfield SJ and James Murphy SJ. My gratitude to my colleague Claire Reid, whose insight that 'writing was a kind of therapy for Ignatius' provided me with a new understanding of Ignatius's life. Finally, thanks to my family and friends for their encouragement in general.

Contents

Introduction

When the canonisation of Ignatius was being considered, a Roman beggar was consulted. It's unlikely that he was popular with the great and good of Roman society, but the beggar was someone Ignatius has made an impression on. He described Ignatius as 'the small Spaniard with a limp who smiled a lot'. I think St Ignatius is often obscured by the image of the 'soldier saint'. While this image has merit, it misses the warmth that was very much part of Ignatius's life and character.

On the 500th anniversary of his 'accident' at Pamplona, perhaps now is an appropriate time to revisit Ignatius's life and to reimagine him through the eyes of the Roman beggar. In this booklet, I hope to show you that other 'smiling' side to Ignatius. It is a side that many readers may not know.

This booklet is not meant to be a definitive life of St Ignatius. I will only cover a few years of his life, from his conversion in 1521 to his commencing studies in Paris in 1528. I hope to give you a glimpse into Ignatius's life and encourage greater interest in the subject. I am convinced that everyone has something they can learn from Ignatius!

Fr Arturo Sosa, the current Superior General of the Jesuits, has written to Jesuits all over the world in anticipation of this anniversary saying: 'In 1521, while Ignatius was convalescing at his family home in Loyola from the wound that damaged his leg at the Battle of Pamplona, God brought about his conversion and put him on the road that led to Manresa. Together with our friends and the whole Church, the universal Society wants to remember that privileged moment when the Holy Spirit inspired Ignatius of Loyola in his decision to follow Christ, and to deepen our understanding of this pilgrim way in order to "draw fruit" from it.'

I hope that by reading this booklet, you may 'draw fruit' from Ignatius's life and grow closer to God. For Ignatius, closeness to God was at the core of his being. It motivated every aspect of his life. Perhaps the right place to begin is with a prayer composed by Ignatius, which outlines God's centrality for him. I hope that you will find this prayer, which is taken from the *Spiritual Exercises*, helpful in your reflections throughout this booklet.

The Suscipe

Take, Lord, and receive all my liberty,
my memory, my understanding,
and my entire will,
All I have and call my own.

You have given all to me.
To you, Lord, I return it.

Everything is yours; do with it what you will.
Give me only your love and your grace,
that is enough for me.

1
Ignatius's World (1491–1521)

Historians tend to agree that Ignatius was born in 1491 in the Basque region of Spain, the year before Columbus made his voyage to the Americas. The European arrival in the Americas was an earthshattering event. It was the dawn of a new age in Europe. New artistic techniques and the 'rediscovery' of classical Rome and Greece were sparking the emergence of what is now called the Renaissance. In many ways, these changes were in marked contrast to the world Ignatius grew up in, which owed more to the Middle Ages than what was happening elsewhere in Europe.

Ignatius's world was that of the court, with kings, princesses and chivalry. Even the religious debates that shattered the unity of the Western Church were not part of Ignatius's early life. The Catholic monarchs Isabella and Ferdinand embarked on a series of reforms within the Spanish Church, many of which would later be adopted by the Council of Trent (1545–63). Their reforms influenced what would come to be called the Counter-Reformation. It is worth noting that there was a good deal of stability in the early life of Ignatius. This stability would not be challenged for the first two decades of his life.

Comfortable people aren't inclined to question their surroundings too much, which was very true of Ignatius. In his *Autobiography*, which he dictated to one of his companions and throughout which he refers to himself in the third person, Ignatius said about his early life, 'Up to his twenty-sixth year he was a man given to worldly vanities, and having a vain and overpowering desire to gain renown'. In life, it is easy to think of times when I have been preoccupied with myself and have concentrated exclusively on personal gain. For Ignatius, this took the shape of being fêted in his courtly world. Today, it might be a promotion at work, a new car, or a holiday home in Spain – something that might give exterior satisfaction but may not produce inner fulfilment.

Ignatius was an outward-looking young man who seems to have given little attention to his relationship with God. Given the nature of religious practice at the time, it can be assumed that he practised his faith in the superficial way expected of people within the courtly world. Religious observance was part of his life, but it is not known what kind of relationship he had with God before his conversion. Given Ignatius's preoccupation with his quest for fame, it is likely that God did not get much attention from him, except perhaps that Ignatius might have prayed to be showered with glory and prestige. Everyone can relate to moments in life when the focus was on what God can do for me, rather than what I can do for God.

Time to Reflect

Looking at Ignatius's life during this early period might help you to reflect on where you are right now in your life. Perhaps this is a good point to pause and ask some questions:

1. How do I relate to God? If I practise my faith, do I do so because I think it is expected of me, or do I desire to have a more personal encounter with God?

2. Am I preoccupied with bettering myself materially? When I pray, what do I pray for most often? Do I focus on what I want from God, or do I ask God to be shown what I can do to serve others?

3. What about the early life of Ignatius matches up with where I am in life? Is this a bad thing or a good thing?

2
The Battle of Pamplona
(May 1521)

The Church has many saints who were soldiers, such as Joan of Arc. Ignatius is often associated with the image of a soldier. It is ironic that so much emphasis is placed on his life as a soldier. Much of his early life was dedicated to what would have been called chivalry, not soldiering. Such a life involved mixing with the rich and powerful, enjoying the finer things that life had to offer and going into battle when necessary. Ignatius did mix with the rich and powerful and it seems he also indulged in the finer things of life, but he only had to go into battle once.

The life of a soldier in Ignatius's time was far from glamorous. It was mostly confined to the poorer classes, who were obliged by feudal loyalties to fight for their masters or who sold their services for money as mercenaries. Their lot in life was very far removed from the world Ignatius was born into. Compared to Joan of Arc, Ignatius's military prowess was relatively limited. Much of his life before the Battle of Pamplona was lived out in service rather than in combat. In a modern context, a courtier was something akin to a groupie attached to a rock band, who loyally follows the group. In Ignatius's time, the court would have travelled around surveying their domains, and Ignatius would have followed accordingly.

While Ignatius might not have been a soldier as you or I know it, military matters certainly played an essential part in his frame of reference. In his *Spiritual Exercises*, Ignatius relies on military analogies to bring his meditations to life. He talks about battle standards, armies, the storming of fortresses, and so on. Such imagery would have been familiar to him. These things sparked his youthful imagination in a way similar to what science-fiction does for young people in today's culture. I am sure had Ignatius been an accountant by profession, this background would have influenced the imagery within the *Spiritual Exercises*. While I am not trying to do away with the image of Ignatius as a soldier, I think a little context is necessary.

> **In his Spiritual Exercises, Ignatius relies on military analogies to bring his meditations to life. ... Such imagery would have been familiar to him.**

Ignatius's world was one where the monarchies of Europe regularly contested one another for power and territory. These contests were often played out by the more prominent countries like France or Spain, who interfered in smaller kingdoms, such as Navarre, which bordered France and an emerging Spain, interfering in smaller kingdoms, such as Navarre, which bordered France and the emerging Spanish kingdom (the marriage of Isabella of

Castile and Ferdinand of Aragon in 1469 would see much of the Iberian Peninsula united under their rulership, and eventually, these territories became Spain). For over ten years, the Spanish fought to gain control of the Iberian portion of Navarre. An important location in this struggle was the town of Pamplona, which was contested by both sides numerous times. The most famous of these clashes came in 1521 when the Navarrese and French tried to recapture the city.

In May 1521 Pamplona was held by forces loyal to the Spanish crown. Amongst those charged with the defence of the town was Ignatius of Loyola. The garrison commander quickly realised that defending Pamplona would not be easy and that it might be more prudent to abandon the city and fight another day. The impetuous Ignatius was horrified at the thought of avoiding a fight. As I mentioned earlier, this was Ignatius's first real experience of battle, so he was probably more focused on making a name for himself than the practicalities of combat. The young Ignatius must have possessed some charm because he convinced the commander that the town should be defended.

In the *Autobiography*, Ignatius confirms the hopelessness of the situation which faced the defenders: 'while everyone else clearly saw that they could not defend themselves and thought that they should surrender to save their lives, he offered so many reasons to the fortress' commander that he talked him into defending it. Though this was contrary to the opinion of all other knights, still each drew encouragement from his firmness and fearlessness'.

Ignatius's honied words were not enough to help the defenders overcome their enemies, they were quickly overwhelmed and the battle ended in a few days.

Ignatius's strong-headed behaviour did not just result in the fall of Pamplona to the invaders, it also resulted in his being injured. At some point in the battle, a cannonball shattered his leg. In the grander scale of things this seemed a relatively minor event, but it was perhaps the most significant moment in the battle, one which would profoundly impact the history of the world. He describes the event in the *Autobiography*, 'a cannonball hit him in a leg, shattering it completely, and since the ball passed between both legs the other one was likewise severely wounded'. He adds that his injury resulted in his comrades deciding to surrender the fortress.

It must have been a strange moment in Ignatius's life. Here was his moment of glory. His confidence had compelled him to ignore all sensible advice and instead rush into a foolhardy gamble. Given his supreme self-belief, it is likely he thought that his heroic words and spirit would be able to bring about victory. Instead, he was shot down in his prime, and the fortress he had sought to save fell to the enemy. It is not known what Ignatius thought about his actions being the cause of others losing their lives unnecessarily. He does not comment on such feelings in the *Autobiography*, but one can assume a good deal of mental anguish accompanied his physical pain.

Time to Reflect

This incident is the most significant moment in this story, so take some time to reflect upon what you have just read:

1. Can you recall a moment when you were so confident that you thought you could achieve anything, but for one reason or another, things did not work out? How did you respond subsequently?

2. Imagine yourself as a soldier with Ignatius in the fortress. What has he said, which has inspired you to stay and fight? Alternatively, what do you say to convince him that now is not the time to fight?

3. In moments of unexpected tragedy, where do you find God, or do you find it hard to relate to God when things do not appear to be working out?

3
Ignatius Returns to Loyola
(June 1521)

It must have been a sign of the respect Ignatius's foes had for him, that they carried him back to his family home after the battle. One can imagine how they admired his courage for having fought, despite the overwhelming odds against him. Ignatius spoke about this in the *Autobiography*, 'after they gained control, [they] treated the wounded man very well, showing him courtesy and kindness. After being in Pamplona for some fifteen days they transported him home on a litter to his home country'. Given the rudimentary nature of roads at the time and the mountainous terrain of northern Spain, the journey must have been torture for Ignatius, who was still suffering from his battle wounds.

By the time he reached his brother's home, Ignatius had said his condition was 'serious'. One can assume this adjective might not be sufficient to capture the level of damage that was done, and the pain Ignatius was going through. From Ignatius's testimony, it is clear that his wounded leg had not been well set when he was at Pamplona, and the journey home is sure to have exacerbated the damage further. As a result of this, his leg was now out of joint and would never heal correctly. While he underwent what he describes as 'butchery' to resolve the problem, the surgeries were unsuccessful and did more harm than good. Without any aesthetic, Ignatius would have been fully aware of the pain that resulted from these operations.

His family feared that he would die, and consequently, he received the Last Rites. During this period, Ignatius turned in prayer to St Peter, to whom he had a special devotion and from the Feast of Ss Peter and Paul, his condition would begin to improve. Ignatius would later attribute this healing to the intercession of St Peter. His torture was not yet over, his leg wound looked unsightly, and for a man still attached to worldly pleasures this deformity repulsed him. Consequently, he asked the doctor to try and undertake a cosmetic procedure on his leg, in the hope of rectifying the problem.

Ignatius describes the gory details and motivation for this operation in his *Autobiography*, 'When the bones did knit together, the one below the knee rested on top of the other so the leg was shortened and the bone so protruded that it made an unsightly bump. Because he was determined to make a way for himself in the world, he could not tolerate such ugliness and thought it marred his appearance. Thus he instructed the surgeon to remove it, if possible. They told him that it could certainly be sawn away, but the pain would be greater than any he had suffered up to now, since the leg had healed and it would take some time to remove the bump. Nevertheless, he was determined to endure this martyrdom to satisfy his personal taste.'

Here a pattern of behaviour emerges. Ignatius was unable to listen to advice from people who might have known better. This could be seen first at Pamplona, where he wanted to fight even though the chances of winning were non-existent. Then, despite nearly dying as a result of his wounds, he was willing to undergo more significant pain to satisfy his vanity. In both cases, Ignatius puts aside the wisdom of others and concentrates on his quest for personal glory. He was willing to lose a battle because he might win and be hailed a hero. He was willing to undergo a painful cosmetic procedure to fit into the fashionable tights men wore in those days, so that he wasn't perceived to be ugly. In everything he did, he had only his own interests at heart. Other people didn't matter to him.

The surgery was as painful as the doctor had predicted. The ointments provided to heal him and medieval devices attached to stretch the leg only exacerbated the pain. Consequently, Ignatius was unable to stand on his leg for some time and found himself confined to bed. Providence begins to take root at this point in Ignatius's story. Up until the Battle of Pamplona, Ignatius was always in command and was the master of his own choices. Confined to bed, he found his ability to control things diminished. As a result, he had to begin to rely on his family for support in the day-to-day things, but more importantly, he began to turn his attention towards God and start working on his interior life. Ignatius's physical healing would be accompanied by spiritual healing.

Being sick in bed is rarely a pleasant experience. Anyone who has spent time in bed recuperating can relate to the intense boredom that accompanies being confined to bed. During such a period distractions are essential. Nowadays, someone might console themselves by binging one of their favourite programs on Netflix. Such modern pleasures were not available in Ignatius's day, and the limited availability of printed books meant that his choices of reading were limited. Hoping to pass some time, Ignatius requested some popular fiction works, which could feed his imagination and spur him onto future glories. Unfortunately for him, the family home didn't have what he was looking for – they could only provide religious books.

The two books given to Ignatius were the *Life of Christ* and the *Lives of the Saints*. It can be taken for granted that Ignatius was sufficiently catechised by the standards of his day. From the incident where he prayed to St Peter, it can also be seen that he had some level of religious devotion. However, for the first time in his life, Ignatius enjoyed a prolonged period alone with Jesus and the saints. The latter book, the *Lives of the Saints*, appears to have made a particular influence upon Ignatius. He found himself very drawn to Ss Francis and Dominic's stories, founders of two important religious orders within the Church.

The attraction to these two saints is noted in his *Autobiography*, 'While reading the life of our Lord and those saints, he used to pause and meditate, reasoning to himself: "What if I were to do what Saint Francis did, or to do what Saint Dominic did?" Thus in his thoughts he dwelt on many good deeds, always suggesting to himself great and difficult ones, but as soon as he considered doing them, they all appeared easy of performance. Throughout these thoughts he used say to himself: "Saint Dominic did this, so I have to do it too. Saint Francis did this, so I have to do it too." These thoughts lasted a long time.'

Ignatius notes that the more he thought about Dominic and Francis's experiences, the less relevant his daydreaming of chivalric glory became. He began to pay attention to how these thoughts began to make him feel. The old dreams of glory in battle or winning the affection of a suitable woman, which once occupied his thoughts, now left him feeling empty. When he reflected on the saints' achievements, he found their accolades very attractive, and he wanted to emulate their deeds in his own life. A transformation had begun in the life of Ignatius. Through reflection, he began to see the deficiencies of his old desires and the life-giving fulfilment that could arise from following in the footsteps of the saints.

Time to Reflect

A lot has happened to Ignatius in this section, so perhaps now is a good time to think about a few questions arising from what you've just read:

1. Throughout the history of the Church, people have been inspired by the lives of holy men and women. The American mystic, Thomas

Merton, after a long period of wrestling about converting to Catholicism, finally took the step to do so after reading about the poet and priest, Gerard Manley Hopkins. Perhaps in your life, some holy man or woman has made a similar impact. If so, take some time to reflect upon this person and how they sparked a transformation in your life.

2. By reading Ignatius formed a connection with Jesus and the saints. This connection was to form the backbone of his life. Is there a book you have read in your life which has had such an impact? If so, take some time to recall how this book influenced your life.

3. Reflecting on your thoughts is an integral part of the Ignatian experience. How often do you take the time to examine your daydreams? Perhaps take some time to do so and afterwards see how you feel. Do they leave you satisfied or are you left wanting more?

4
A Time of Change
(June 1521–February 1522)

The change that took place in Ignatius was profound, but his former way of life still attracted him. For so long, his quest for glory had encompassed everything in his life. He could hardly just walk away from these thoughts and start anew. A battle raged within him, while he found consolation from old thoughts. His former ambitions still tried to entice his imagination. Anyone making a change in their life knows that the hardest period is early on, when the comfort of where you have come from can seem very attractive compared to the path you have sought to embark on. This was no different for Ignatius, who wrestled with a variety of competing desires.

It is at this point in Ignatius's life that he records his first mystical experience, which can be found in his *Autobiography*, 'One night, as he lay sleepless, he clearly saw the likeness of our Lady with the holy Child Jesus, and because of this vision he enjoyed an excess of consolation for a remarkably long time. He felt so great a loathsomeness for all his past life … that it seemed to him that all the images that had been previously imprinted on his mind were now erased.'

In Ignatian terms, this was a moment of consolation. Ignatius was able to differentiate this event from the ones that had come before and deduce that he was moving in the right direction. Whether or not Ignatius had had previous mystical experiences, it is clear that with this experience he was beginning to take charge of his life and move in a new direction. Few people will have mystical experiences of this nature, but this does not mean that you cannot take the time to weigh up your thoughts and discern what God is calling you to do. In doing so, you can learn to separate what is helpful in that direction as opposed to what prevents you from growing closer to God.

This incident with Our Lady helped to increase Ignatius's growing attraction to contemplation. The *Autobiography* tells that he began to write down things that struck him in the books he read. As well as reading, Ignatius began to have spiritual conversations with the people living in his brother's house. He found that he received much consolation from these interactions. He notes something worth mentioning in the *Autobiography*. During this period he began to get attracted to looking towards the heavens, he says, 'The greatest consolation he received at this time was from gazing at the sky and stars, and this he did for quite a long time. The result of all this was that he felt within himself a strong impulse to serve the Lord'.

Here is an amazing example of how much this period had transformed Ignatius's life. Contrast the chivalric courtier who concerned himself with self-advancement with an Ignatius quiet in contemplation, looking at the stars. A life that was once so full of noise has now been replaced by something simple. His satisfaction now came from something so pure – looking at the stars – and from this Ignatius derived great pleasure and a sense of peace.

At this point, Ignatius began to consider entering religious life. There is a certain irony given the apostolic nature of the order he eventually founded, that Ignatius was initially attracted to life as a Carthusian. The Carthusians are a strict order that operates almost entirely in silence. The monks live in independent cells within their communities and spending their days working and praying in silence. Such a life seems very distant from that of a Jesuit; the missionary spirit seems very much at odds with the Carthusian experience. However, both orders have at their roots the essential desire to find God and for each member to live out their life as God demands. From some, God requests silence, and for others missionary zeal.

> **A life that was once so full of noise has now been replaced by something simple. His satisfaction now came from something so pure – looking at the stars – and from this Ignatius derived great pleasure and a sense of peace.**

The attraction to Carthusian life dimmed for Ignatius, but never wholly left him. When he had put aside an immediate desire to enter the Carthusians, he wondered what he would do to serve God. After long contemplation and recovery in his brother's house, he knew the answers to this question would have to be sought elsewhere. Consequently, Ignatius was to set off to find where God was calling him in the world.

Ignatius's family could see that he was a changed man. These changes startled his worldly brother. When he announced that he was leaving and planned to collect some money owed to him by a nobleman, his brother requested that some servants travel with him. Ignatius left his family home after nine months in recovery and set out for Navarrete. En-route Ignatius stopped off at the chapel of Arantzazu, where he spent the night in prayer before a statue of Our Lady. Here Ignatius made a personal vow of chastity, a big step for the former womaniser. An all-night prayer vigil was in marked contrast to what he would have done previously and must have confused the servants accompanying him.

When Ignatius eventually collected his money, he paid off all his outstanding debts and used the remainder to refurbish a statute of Our Lady. With this job complete, Ignatius dismissed his brother's servants and set out alone. Riding on a mule, Ignatius planned to make his way to Saragossa. As he was travelling, Ignatius encountered a fellow traveller, and he struck up a conversation with him. The man was a Muslim, and given Ignatius's newfound zeal, their conversation turned to religious matters. At some point in their discussion, the topic of the perpetual virginity of Mary arose. The Muslim admitted he could believe in the virgin birth, but did not think Mary remained a virgin after Jesus was born.

Ignatius took great offense at this suggestion, and his chivalric instincts began to kick in. He felt that Mary's honour had been besmirched and that the only thing that he could do to correct this was to kill the man who dishonoured her. In our time, such a train of thought is shocking, it is important to remember that honour and vengeance were a central part of Ignatius's cultural context. He discusses the process of his subsequent discernment (a spiritual practice of decision-making) in the *Autobiography*. 'Tired of trying to figure out what would be the good thing to do, and unable to come to any definitive decision, he determined on the following, namely, to give the mule free rein and to let it go by itself to the point where the roads met. If the mule took the road to the village, he would then search out the Moor and use his dagger on him; if the mule took the highway and not the village road, he would let the Moor go.'

As it transpired, the mule did not go into the village and chose to take the other path. It doesn't bear to think about what would have happened if the mule decided to follow the road into the village. This incident, recounted by Ignatius, may be a strange moment in his story. It certainly isn't an example of a method for discernment. If there is anything to learn from this, it is that Ignatius was not fully converted at this point. The courtier's instincts were still lurking within him, and while great strides had been made to change his ways, Ignatius had to become aware that God was still not finished transforming his life. Ignatius could not afford to become complacent.

Time to Reflect

A great deal has now happened in the life of Ignatius, so pause and take some time to reflect on what you have read:

1. What have you learned about discernment from what you've read so far? Can you think of discernments in your own life and what tactics you used to make a decision?

2. Our Lady plays an essential part in the story of Ignatius. Take some time to read John 2:1–11. Mary points the way to Jesus, how do you see Mary doing the same in the life of Ignatius? Perhaps Mary has helped you draw closer to Jesus too?

3. At this point in the story, what are your thoughts regarding Ignatius? Take some time to think about how you feel about him. Do you find that you like him or does thinking about him create feelings of frustration?

5
The Monastery of Montserrat
(March 1522)

Arriving in the monastery of Montserrat, Ignatius had concluded that he would travel to Jerusalem. He purchased sackcloth and began to carry a pilgrim's staff in preparation for his journey. Jerusalem was the pinnacle point of any Christian journey. The desire to walk in the footsteps of Jesus was as insatiable in Ignatius's time as it might be for anyone today. For a man with such an active imagination, Ignatius would have loved the idea of seeing and experiencing the same landscapes as Jesus and incorporating these scenes into his prayer life. Jerusalem was to become a significant part of Ignatius's life and motivations for many years to come.

Ignatius was very motivated by the spiritual books that he read. However, when coming to Montserrat, Ignatius noted that he was inspired by *Amadís of Gaula*, a piece of fiction popular in his time. The book is filled with stories of knights and chivalry, and it was a source of inspiration for Ignatius. Having had such an appreciation for the chivalric life, it is hard to imagine that such thoughts would have left Ignatius's mind quickly. Being a knight for

Christ began to animate Ignatius's thinking at Montserrat. Like the courtly knights who made vigils before being invested, Ignatius intended to do the same himself; he too would have an all-night vigil. Ignatius's vigil would take place before the statue of the Black Madonna at the altar of Our Lady of Montserrat.

In his book on Ignatius, *Alone and on Foot*, Brian Grogan notes: 'for the knights' vigil of alms is not designed for amusement, nor for anything like that, but to beg God to protect them … as men entering a career of death'. The vigil was serious business for Ignatius and you can be sure that he devoted the night to intense prayer. In the *Autobiography*, Ignatius recounts the vigil, 'he offered prayer and arranged for a confessor. He made a general confession in writing, which lasted three days, and arranged with his confessor to leave his mule behind and to hang his sword and dagger at our Lady's altar in the church. The confessor was the first man to whom he revealed his plans, for up to now he had never told them to any confessor.'

Before the Black Madonna statue, Ignatius laid down his sword; the weapon of the knight had been put aside, and he took up the pilgrim stick in its place.

Before the Black Madonna statue, Ignatius laid down his sword; the weapon of the knight had been put aside, and he took up the pilgrim stick in its place. He had begun his life on the road and his journey towards a greater knowledge of God and how God was active in his life. Ignatius also decided to give away his fine clothes to a local beggar he met around Montserrat. This act of kindness resulted in a hostile encounter for the begging man and is recounted in the *Autobiography*, 'After he travelled about a league from Montserrat, a man who had been pursuing him caught up with him and asked if he had given some clothing to a certain poor man as the poor man claimed. As he answered that he had done so, tears of compassion rolled from his eyes on behalf of the man to whom he had given his clothes – tears of compassion because he realised that the man was now being suspected of having stolen them.'

This incident is an interesting one. Ignatius comments upon his feelings in response to the incident. If you think back to Ignatius's early life, you will remember that he lived only for himself and did not take into account the feelings of others. His personal ambition was something which came before the feelings and opinions of other people. Ignatius's tears are an external sign of his internal transformation. His planned pilgrimage to Jerusalem is running consecutively with the interior pilgrimage that will bring him closer to God and other people.

Ignatius was moved by what had happened to him at Montserrat and would need time to process what he had experienced. Consequently, he would go to Manresa rather than head directly to Jerusalem.

Time to Reflect

Many things are changing for Ignatius, even though some things remain the same. Now is a good time to pause and reflect:

1. Ignatius was inspired by *Amadís of Gaula*. Can you think of something that inspires you in your life in the same way?

2. Ignatius's empathy for the beggar at Montserrat marks a significant change in how he relates to people, have you ever put your personal ambition before the feelings of others?

3. There are experiences that are overwhelming, do you take time in your life to process what you have experienced during the day?

6
Ignatius at Manresa
(25 March 1522–February 1523)

Manresa has an essential place in Jesuit vocabulary. It is a place of beginnings. My novitiate building was named Manresa because this was a point of origin for new Jesuits. The Irish province retreat house is also called Manresa, this too can be a place for new beginnings, but can also be the place where people can reconnect to the source and summit of their lives. For Ignatius, his time in Manresa would be a chance for these things to happen. Not only would he perfect his relationship with God, but he would also formulate his spiritual thoughts, which would later become the basis of his *Spiritual Exercises*.

Coming to Manresa, Ignatius was to encounter one of his most devoted female friends, Inés Pascual. Inés Pascual was to become a major supporter and benefactor of Ignatius and the early Jesuits. Inés's children would later attest to Ignatius's holiness during his canonisation process. These connections with Inés and her family were to be the nucleus of Ignatius and his lay companions. While many people may know Ignatius for his founding of the Jesuits, they may be unaware that he cultivated and maintained friendships with laypeople, in particular women, with whom he communicated throughout his life. These friendships were to play an essential part in Ignatius discerning that other people had a share in his mission. This interaction with other people, and the necessity of sharing his mission, is something that will become clearer as Ignatius's story progresses.

Ignatius's time in Manresa was marked by his awareness of how he was affected by the Good and Evil Spirit. Today talk of spirits might seem outdated, however, it was an integral part of Ignatius's spirituality and was to form the cornerstone of his *Spiritual Exercises*. At Manresa, Ignatius began to chat about how he was plagued by the Evil Spirit, which at times made him feel happy and at other times drove him to the point of suicide. In today's over-psychologised world, it is tempting to try and diagnose what Ignatius was going through. It is more faithful to the spirit of his writings to examine what he was experiencing within a mystical context.

Ignatius believed that the human person was open to the influences of God and the devil. For Ignatius, God – employing the Holy Spirit – drew people towards faith, hope and charity. Ignatius sometimes refers to this as the 'Good Spirit'. Alternatively, the devil, using sinister machinations, causes people to fall into a false sense of self. This can be done in a variety of ways: false consolation might make someone believe they had achieved something worthwhile but the fruit of this achievement would be unsatisfying, pangs of doubt might be employed to crush someone and leave them feeling dejected.

The most concrete example of Ignatius's thinking around the topic can be found within his *Spiritual Exercises*. Here Ignatius gives what he calls 'rules' for understanding the Good and Evil Spirit. For Ignatius, the key to these rules is to move closer to God and reject what is evil. Ignatius's advice is practical and was born out of the time he spent in Manresa. Early in his stay in Manresa, Ignatius began to experience false consolation, which he talks about in his *Autobiography*, 'Up to this time he continued undisturbed in the same interior state of great and constant joy without knowing anything about internal spiritual matters. During the days that the vision lasted … a disturbing thought came to torment him, pointing out to him the burdensomeness of his life. It was like someone speaking within his soul: "And how will you be able to put up with this for the seventy years ahead of you?" Perceiving that this was the voice of the enemy, he likewise interiorly answered and with great courage: "Oh you wretch! Can you promise me one hour of life?" Thus he overcame the temptation and remained tranquil.'

> Ignatius gives what he calls 'rules' for understanding the Good and Evil Spirit. For Ignatius, the key to these rules is to move closer to God and reject what is evil.

Here is a textbook example of the discernment of spirits. Firstly, there is a sense of false consolation. This is a consolation that doesn't last very long past the moment it is experienced. Therefore, the fruit of the moment is not sustainable or satisfying. Secondly, there is a realisation that this is not coming from the Good Spirit, and it can be cited as an example of false consolation. In Ignatius's case, the Evil Spirit causes him to despair and question the futility of having a long life ahead of him. In response, Ignatius is ready to challenge the Evil Spirit and highlight the falsehood of his reasoning, and thus he returns to a more tranquil state of being.

In an attempt to abandon his past vainglory, Ignatius began to neglect his physical appearance. This was done to demonstrate an external break with his past obsessions with self-image, however, at Manresa, he experienced new insights around this practice. He states in his *Autobiography*, 'after experiencing divine consolations and seeing the fruit he was bringing forth in the souls he was helping, he abandoned those extremes he had previously practiced and began to cut his nails and hair.'

This example gives insight into the spiritual movements that were taking place within Ignatius. Before Manresa, he was still preoccupied with the outer self. This was very manifest in how he allowed his physical appearance to decline. In doing this, he was setting up something for other people to contemplate rather than something that helps promote inner growth and strengthens the relationship with God. By maintaining a shabby outer experience to make up for his past excessive grooming Ignatius was only demonstrating something external, the real work of conversion happens interiorly, and this realisation happened for him at Manresa.

These discoveries were invaluable to the formation of Ignatius's spirituality. Manresa was perhaps the greatest school Ignatius ever attended and he attests to this in his *Autobiography*, 'During this period God was dealing with him in the same way a school teacher deals with a child while instructing him. This was either because he was thick and dull of brain or because of the firm will that God Himself had implanted in him to serve Him – but clearly recognized and has always recognised that it was in this way God dealt with him.'

Ignatius's language here is self-deprecating and highlights how wilful he was in responding to God's interactions with him. At this point, Ignatius was still undecided as to what God was calling him to do with his life. It was this question that had drawn him from his family home and brought him to Manresa. In trying to figure out what God was calling him to do Ignatius managed to gain a great insight on how to discern the movement of spirits. While this experience caused him some hardship, it ensured that he was able to provide concrete examples for people in future who were experiencing the same thing.

Ignatius's Spirituality

A great deal is said about Ignatian spirituality in religious circles today, but it often bears little resemblance to what motivated Ignatius. Ignatius had a profound relationship with the three persons of the Holy Trinity, Our Lady and the Saints, some of which are not in vogue with modern devotees of Ignatian spirituality. Thus, it is essential to look at the kind of mysticism that captured Ignatius's heart while he was at Manresa, in particular his experience of the Holy Trinity. These mystical movements give further insights into what Ignatius was going through, but also they allow you to gain an understanding of his later spiritual writing.

The Holy Trinity captured the imagination of Ignatius. In his *Spiritual Exercises*, he introduces prayerful meditations that include the three persons of the Trinity. In one such meditation, he envisions the three persons of the Trinity contemplating the world and deciding the time was opportune to send the Son, Jesus, into the world. To his meditations, Ignatius adds what he calls a 'colloquy'. In these Ignatius invites the retreatant to enter into conversations with the three persons of the Trinity to gain greater insights about their interior movements. For Ignatius, his entire spirituality was wrapped in a blanket of Trinitarianism that shaped how he interacted with the divine.

> **Ignatius was very much a man of his time and deeply attached to the piety and customs that he was exposed to.**

This understanding of and attachment to the Holy Trinity finds its roots in his time at Manresa and a mystical moment that Ignatius experienced. Ignatius describes this mystical moment in the *Autobiography*, 'One day he was saying the Hours of Our Lady on the monastery's steps, his understanding was raised on high, so as to see the Most Holy Trinity under the aspect of three keys on a musical instrument, and as a result he shed many tears and sobbed so strongly that he could not control himself ... he could not hold back the tears until dinnertime, and after he had eaten he could not refrain from talking, with much joy and consolation, about the Most Holy Trinity, making use of different comparisons. This experience remained with him for the rest of his life, so that whenever he prayed to the Most Holy Trinity he felt great devotion.'

This gives an insight into how Ignatius prayed. Devotional material like the *Little Office of the Blessed Virgin Mary* influenced his prayer life. Such material would have been commonly available to the laity in Ignatius's time and allowed them to experience the psalms, hymns and scripture readings. Ever since his bedridden conversion, Ignatius was very attached to the saints and like many people of his time he placed great faith in their intercession. This did not mean they acted in place of God, far from it, but rather their prayers acted in unison with those of the faithful in reaching God. Ignatius was very much a man of his time and deeply attached to the piety and customs that he was exposed to.

Central to Ignatius's spirituality was the eucharist. As someone who was always seeking to grow closer to Christ, Ignatius placed great stock in the eucharist. For his time he was enlightened as to how he approached reception of the sacrament. In the medieval Church, communion was infrequent, most people only went to communion twice a year, usually at Christmas and Easter. The practice of irregular communion remained relatively normal until the early twentieth century when Pope Pius X extolled the value of frequent communion. Ignatius was ahead of his time, receiving weekly communion and encouraging others to do the same.

It was at Manresa he began to gain his most significant understanding of the eucharist, as is recorded in his *Autobiography*, 'he saw with his inward eyes, at the time of elevation of the Body of the Lord, some white ray coming from above … he clearly saw with his understanding how our Lord Jesus Christ was present in that Most Holy Sacrament.'

The centrality of Jesus in Ignatius's life cannot be underestimated. Jesus, the sacraments, the Saints, Our Lady and the other persons in Holy Trinity are the core of what was Ignatius's spirituality. All these things enriched how he saw God at work in the world and nourished God's closeness to human beings. It gave Ignatius the tools he needed to formulate his *Spiritual Exercises* and allowed him to become a gifted conversationalist and director on spiritual matters. The revolutionary gift for Ignatius was not that he discovered anything new but that he looked deeply into what was around him and came to a greater understanding of God, which he then freely shared with others.

By the Banks of the Cardoner

The most significant moment for Ignatius during his time at Manresa took place at the River Cardoner. Sitting by the river, Ignatius underwent his most profound mystical experience, which was recorded in his *Autobiography*, 'he sat down facing the river far below him. As he sat there the eyes of his understanding were opened, and though he saw no vision, he understood and perceived many things, numerous spiritual things as well as matters touching on faith and learning, and this was with an elucidation so bright that all these things seemed new to him. He cannot expound in detail what he then understood, for there were many things, but he can state that he received such a lucidity that during the course of his entire life – now having passed his sixty-second year – if he were to gather all the helps he received from God and everything he knew, and add them together, he does not think they would add up to all that he received on that one occasion.'

Mystical moments such as this are relatively rare in the human experience and often set the tone for the rest of someone's life. Thomas Aquinas, after years of formulating great philosophical and theological ideas, underwent a mystical vision, and declared all his previous work was like 'straw' compared to what had happened to him. He died shortly after, never writing another word of philosophy or theology. Thankfully, Ignatius did not follow the example of Thomas Aquinas and did not cease his output as a result of his Cardoner vision. Instead, this incident was to be the central moment in his life and would help propel him from Manresa and onward on his journey.

Time to Reflect

Ignatius's year at Manresa was challenging and transformative for his spiritual life. Now is a good time to reflect on your own spiritual life:

1. Where do you draw nourishment from?

2. How has your relationship with God changed over time? Be sure to stop at the significant spiritual moments in your life and explore what God was saying to you at that time. Like Ignatius, it might be helpful to write down your own experiences to assist you in processing them.

7
Interlude in Italy
(March 1523–July 1523)

Ignatius left Manresa and walked to Barcelona, where he planned to travel to Rome and receive the necessary documentation to enter the Holy Land. Ignatius's voyage from Barcelona to the Italian peninsula took five days, and the ship would land at Gaeta, a port 140 kilometres south of Rome. This meant Ignatius would have to walk to Rome, which was something he was becoming accustomed to. On reaching Rome he received the necessary documents that would allow him entry into the Holy Land, and he also received a blessing from Pope Adrian VI. From Rome, Ignatius had to travel to Venice, where he would sail to the Holy Land. This is a journey of 526 kilometres and would take Ignatius through a variety of different cities, towns and territories.

At this time Italy was not a united country as it is today; Italy was a collection of city-states and more extensive territories, and travelling through these areas could be difficult. Spanish attempts to assert their control over parts of the Italian peninsula made Spanish travellers a target of hostility, so this was something Ignatius would have been conscious of as he journeyed to Venice. Ignatius records in his *Autobiography* that he did not have the relevant documentation he needed to pass through specific places on many occasions, so he had to hand himself over to God's providence continually. Luckily he managed to make his way to Venice without being denied entry anywhere en-route.

Upon arriving in Venice, Ignatius begged around the city and slept in St Mark's Square. At some point, he decided that he must travel to the Holy Land on providence. This meant he would rely on God rather than on money he had accumulated from begging or by another person's paying his way. Such a circumstance seemed unrealistic to Ignatius's listeners, who felt that this would not happen. While in Venice, Ignatius notes that he met 'a rich Spaniard' who invited him to his home. Here you can catch a glimpse of how Ignatius engaged with people and why he was so sought after for counsel. In the *Autobiography* he writes, 'Ever since his days in Manresa the pilgrim had the custom, when he was eating with others, of never talking at table, except to give brief answers. But he listened to all that was said and mentally noted certain items that he would later use in speaking about God.'

This passage demonstrates skills Ignatius would deploy in how he engaged with all kinds of people. Many people find a shortage of attentive listeners in their own lives. When you are listening to someone, you might find that you have already decided what they will say while the other person is still talking! In that sense, you are not really listening and actively picking up on what the other person is saying. You fail to hear them. This communication breakdown can mean that the relationship suffers and neither party is satisfied with the other.

Ignatius takes a different approach. Ignatius listens to everything you say with future spiritual conversations in mind. Rather than focus on how he will answer you, Ignatius takes time to contemplate the meaning behind what you are saying. This technique is a significant part of modern spiritual direction, where the director is encouraged to listen more than to speak. Ignatius displays a pioneering spirit in this regard, and it is something that his earlier companions must have learnt from him, and which helped to make them such effective evangelists.

In Venice, this mode of engaging served Ignatius well. The 'rich Spaniard' introduced him to the recently elected Doge of Venice, Andrea Gritti. Hearing of Ignatius's desire to travel to the Holy Land, Gritti gave Ignatius free passage on a government-owned ship travelling to Cyprus. From there, Ignatius would be able to enter the Holy Land. Here was the act of providence Ignatius had sought. An encounter with a wealthy fellow countryman allowed him access to the most influential person in Venice.

Once again, the character of Ignatius is evident in this incident. People were willing to invest in him; they saw something in him, which made them want to be associated with him. On 14 July 1523 Ignatius left Venice for the Holy Land.

Time to Reflect

Providence and an ability to really listen have helped Ignatius on his way to the Holy Land. Now is a good time to pause and consider the role that providence and even the simple ability to listen have played in your life:

1. Providence meant everything to Ignatius. He put total trust in God and believed that if something were to happen, then God would ensure that it would. How much do you trust in providence? Have there ever been periods of your life where you can point to specific moments of God's providence?

2. Active listening is a great skill to have. Ask yourself, are you a good listener? If so, what makes you a good listener, think of some examples. Alternatively, if you struggle to listen to others, how might you improve on hearing what people say?

8
Ignatius in the Holy Land
(September 1523–October 1523)

I n September 1523 Ignatius arrived at the port of
Jaffa. On departing the ship, he sang 'Te Deum' and
'Salve Regina', in thanksgiving for his safe journey. The
Holy Land had long held a special place in the hearts of
Christians, and pilgrims had dreamt of seeing the places
where Jesus had lived and ministered. In 326–28 St
Helena, mother of the emperor Constantine, embarked
on a journey to discover the sites associated with the life
of Jesus. This trip led her to discover what she considered
the True Cross and the Holy Sepulchre site. St Helena's
journey would inspire other Christians to make similar
pilgrimages after that.

The Franciscans were the dominant force of Western
Christianity in the Holy Land and had been since the time
of Francis. Francis himself had passed through the Holy
Land in 1219–1220 and had long envisioned his friars
ministering there. The Franciscans established a custody in
the Holy Land in 1217, which was part of Francis's larger
vision of ministry to every corner of the known world. By
1342 the Papacy had declared the Franciscans the Holy

Land's official custodians and issued two Papal Bulls to this effect. When Ignatius disembarked at Jaffa, he was welcomed by the Franciscans. He would also lodge with them during his time in the Holy Land. Unbeknownst to his Franciscan hosts, Ignatius came with no intention of leaving.

The pilgrims travelled from Jaffa by donkey. As they approached Jerusalem, a fellow pilgrim suggested that they do so in silence and prepare themselves to see the Holy City. Ignatius recounts this moment in his *Autobiography*, 'Since this seemed agreeable to all, each one recollected himself, and a little before they arrived at the place whence they could get a glimpse of the city, they dismounted because they noticed friars waiting for them with a cross. When the pilgrim did see the city, he experienced great consolation, and all others affirmed the same, saying that all felt a joy that did not seem natural. He felt this same devotion on all his visits to the Holy Places.'

Encountering the sites relating to Jesus' life filled Ignatius with great joy and strengthened his resolve to remain in the Holy Land. He had prepared for this before arrival and had solicited approval letters to endorse his credentials as someone worth keeping. In hoping to remain in Jerusalem, Ignatius not only wanted to be amongst the places Jesus visited in his earthy life, but Ignatius planned to 'help souls'. On presenting his letters of recommendation to the Franciscans, he focused on his devotion. He decided to omit to mention his plans to 'help souls'.

Despite his great enthusiasm, the Franciscans were less enticed by the idea of having Ignatius remain in the Holy

Land. They had seen zealous pilgrims arrive in the past, and often it had not ended well. It must be remembered that they were a minority faith surrounded by neighbours who at times could be hostile to their presence. In his *Autobiography*, Ignatius recounts how in the past others who stayed and tried to evangelise the local populace were in some cases killed or kept for ransom. The Franciscans assured him that they were too poor to pay any ransoms which would be demanded of a captive Ignatius. This initial reluctance of the Franciscans did not dissuade Ignatius, and he requested to speak with their provincial (superior of the Franciscan community in the Holy Land).

Upon returning from Bethlehem, the provincial of the Franciscan community agreed to meet with Ignatius. The meeting with the provincial is recounted in Ignatius's *Autobiography*, 'The provincial told him most kindly that he knew of his good intentions to remain in the Holy Places and that he had given much thought on the matter; nevertheless, because of his experience with others he judged it was not a good idea … He replied that his decision to remain was fixed and nothing could prevent him from carrying it out. With great honesty he gave the provincial to understand that though the provincial did not agree with him, and since this was not a matter that obliged under sin, he would not renounce his plans out of fear.'

Ignatius was stubborn in his plans to remain in the Holy Land. All his prayer and desires seemed to point him to this place. He was so convinced of this that he was ready to argue his case, believing this was where God had called him to be. Despite this desire, the Franciscans were immovable in their opposition as Ignatius tells us: 'In answer to him the provincial said that they had authority from the Apostolic See to expel or keep anyone they chose and to excommunicate anyone who refused to obey ... The provincial was willing to show him the bulls empowering him to excommunicate, but he said he had no need to see them since he believed their reverences, and since they arrived at their decision in accordance with the authority they possessed, he would obey them. When this was all over he returned to the place where he was staying, since it was not our Lord's will for him to remain in the Holy Places.'

Ignatius recounts this much later in his life when he is dictating the story to a Jesuit companion. His resignation is total, and if it was so complete and without argument, it is somewhat admirable. It is important to remember Ignatius was drawn to the Holy Land by intense prayer and felt assured this was where God wanted him to be. Not only did he think God was calling him to this place, but that some form of evangelical ministry awaited him amongst the local inhabitants, a plan to 'help souls'. This makes Ignatius's acceptance all the more impressive because he is prepared to forego his own experience and listen to the will of those in possession of more significant facts. From this, he deduced, leaving was the will of God.

What is to be made of this? Does this denigrate Ignatius's own prayer experiences and show that everything before this was misinformation? No, I think God was drawing him to Jerusalem. All of this was formational in Ignatius's life.

By seeing sites connected with Jesus, he gained a greater appreciation of Jesus' ministry and came to understand this as he would meditate on the life of Jesus. This helped to increase and formulate his profound intimacy with Jesus and assist others to do the same. Secondly, it helped him realise that people are not the God-given masters of their own experience in spiritual matters. While you are the sole owner of your prayer experiences, you will sometimes need others to help you formulate what is happening, and to tease out God's will and separate it from your own desires.

Before he left the Holy Land Ignatius tells a touching story about his final visit to a place of pilgrimage, 'On the Mount of Olives there is a stone from which our Lord ascended into heaven, and his footprints are still visible there. This was what he wanted to see … While there he remembered he had not taken full notice of the direction in which the right foot was pointing and which way the left. On his return there he gave scissors, I think, to the guards so that they would let him enter.'

The story is an excellent conclusion to his time in Jerusalem, and it draws him to the reason for being there in the first place, a greater knowledge of Jesus. Those who have experienced Ignatius's Spiritual Exercises know that the life of Jesus is central to them. As Ignatius wrote his meditations on Jesus' life, he was drawing upon his time in the Holy Land. His lived experience of Jesus' earthy home allowed him to understand the environment that shaped Jesus. God wanted Ignatius to see Jerusalem, even if he could not remain there.

Time to Reflect

Ignatius's journey to the Holy Land has been disappointing in some ways, and yet significant in others. Now is a good moment to pause and reflect on your experience of pilgrimage and those times when things don't work out as planned:

1. Pilgrimage is an important part of the spiritual experience. Have you ever gone on pilgrimage? If so take some time to reflect upon the experience. What gifts did God give you during that time? Alternatively, did you experience challenges, and if so, how did you resolve them?

2. Ignatius felt drawn to Jerusalem through his prayer. Have you ever been sure of something that ultimately did not work out as you had planned? If so, can you see God working at that moment and directing you towards some other course in life?

9
Return to Spain and then to Paris
(March 1524–28)

With his plan to stay in Jerusalem now dashed, Ignatius found himself back where he started his journey, Spain. The rejection of the Franciscans meant Ignatius had to reconsider what he would do with his life. In his prayer, Ignatius still felt drawn to 'help souls', but he would have to find a new avenue to make this ambition a reality. Arriving back in Spain, Ignatius set himself up in Barcelona, where he resumed his usual practice of begging for alms and lodging in hospitals with the poor and unwanted.

During this period, Ignatius reconnected with some wealthy women he had met while he was in Manresa, among them was Inés Pascual. In Barcelona, Ignatius found support and encouragement from these women and in return, he provided them with spiritual advice. The oldest remaining letter from Ignatius was to Inés Pascual, and in it, he offered spiritual guidance. This practice of spiritually directing women became a source of suspicion amongst Church authorities. Many questioned what authority Ignatius had to offer spiritual advice. After all, he had no formal education, and such a role was the preserve of the clergy.

The lack of education was something he wanted to correct, and he decided to return to school. At this point, Ignatius was in his mid-thirties and found himself amongst teenage boys, trying to get a better command of Latin, which he would need for future studies. Here was a moment of humility: the once-proud courtier was back in school amongst children and found that this was a struggle academically. He recounts this in his *Autobiography*, 'whenever he tried to memorise anything, as it is necessary in the early stages of Grammarly study, new understandings of spiritual delights came to him, and in such a way that he could neither memorise anything nor could he get rid of them, no matter how much he tried.'

Here Ignatius was becoming distracted by seemingly good things, which made his study laborious and difficult. His primary desire at this time was to study, not to grow in spiritual insights. Thus, Ignatius noted the movement that was taking place within him. While objectively good, Ignatius exposed these 'understandings of spiritual delights' to be the Evil Spirit's tactic. As Ignatius learnt in Manresa, the Evil Spirit will always try to use a seemingly good thing to keep a person from achieving a greater good. Had Ignatius decided to lose interest in his studies and allow his mind to roam to other distractions, it is likely he would have remained uneducated and thus been unable for the purpose God was calling him to.

This period of Ignatius's life coincided with a group known as the Alumbrados (Enlightened ones). These were a group of Christians who were attracted to mysticism and desired a personal connection to God. They believed that when this personal connection happened, all other things became superfluous. They shunned all forms of external worship and believed that sin was irrelevant once they reached the point of mystical connection. The group became a target of suspicion and attracted the attention of the Spanish Inquisition. Ignatius's reputation as a mystic and lack of theological education led to some believing him to be an Alumbrado.

At this time, his simplicity of life had begun to attract followers, who joined in his way of life and catechetical work. Unlike later in his life, these groupings were never formalised and didn't persevere. When he finished two years of studies in Barcelona, he travelled to Alcalá. There he began university studies. In his spare time, he taught children their catechism and had spiritual conversations with adults. His spiritual conversations were based on what would eventually become his *Spiritual Exercises*. Presenting his own interpretation on spiritual matters aroused his detractors' suspicion, and word of this travelled to ecclesial authorities. The accusations led to Ignatius being suspected as an Alumbrado, which got him into trouble with the Spanish Inquisition.

He touches on this period in his *Autobiography*, 'This matter reached the Inquisition in Toledo, and when the inquisitors came to Alcalá the pilgrim was warned by their host, who told him that they were calling them "sack wearers" and "enlightened one". They immediately began an investigation into their lives, but in the end they returned to Toledo without summoning them.'

The investigation by the inquisition was not the end of his trouble. Ignatius and his followers were criticised for their dress and continued teaching. This resulted in his imprisonment for a period of time. A more serious event occurred in Salamanca when he ran foul of the Dominican friars. His writings, which became the *Spiritual Exercises*, came under scrutiny, and Ignatius was put on trial. The occasion caused division in the Dominican community and saw support from people in the city who had come to respect Ignatius. Ignatius's opponents wanted to know whether or not his thinking and writing and were in line with Church teaching.

Writing about the trial Ignatius tells us, 'Then the ordered him to explain the First Commandment as he usually explained it … Their problem was he though uneducated, was determining the question.'

Here was the central point his opponents raised, Ignatius had no right to teach as they saw him as unlearned within the conventions of the day. Once again, he had to decide to make a change in his life. Knowing that the best education in Europe was at that time in Paris, Ignatius decided to set out there, once he was found not guilty at his trial. His close encounters with various Church authorities meant that he would have to get the necessary qualifications to 'help souls' and ultimately become a priest. In 1528 Ignatius left Spain for France, closing the door on his time as a wandering pilgrim. Paris would begin his journey towards founding the Society of Jesus (Jesuits), but that is another story!

10
Three Lessons from Ignatius

Lesson One: Change is OK

Ignatius had his life mapped out for him. He was going to be a soldier. He would win many battles, achieve great glory, and marry the woman of his dreams. God had other plans, though, and the impact of a cannonball not only shattered his leg but left his plans in tatters too. In a world where you are expected to have everything in order and certainty is so important, little room is left for life-changing events. While all change is not necessarily good, you have to make room for change and to explore where it can lead you.

Ignatius did not embrace the change productively at first. His early endeavours were often met with failure and disappointment. His journey to the Holy Land did not turn out the way he wanted. When Ignatius's existing plans didn't work out, he opened himself to exploring change. Over time he came to see that the change that emerged turned out to be beneficial and brought him greater satisfaction than the life that had previously seemed so certain.

Lesson Two: Community is Vital

After his religious conversion, Ignatius came to realise that the insights God was giving him had to be shared, and he sought out likeminded people. Much of his early ministry was focused on the sharing of his *Spiritual Exercises* with various women – like Inés Pascual – who would form the financial and prayerful backbone of the Society of Jesus (Jesuits). Ignatius's voluminous correspondences contain many letters to these women, showing how their friendship and prayers motivated him into greater service of God.

Ignatius understood the importance of getting help along the way. His ability to listen and his openness to others helped him form relationships with people – like the wealthy Spaniard and the Doge of Venice – who could help on his pilgrim journey. He learned to listen to others even when they were telling him what he didn't want to hear. Unlike at the Battle of Pamplona, in the Holy Land Ignatius listened to those around him, especially the Franciscan provincial.

His apostolic zeal was strong, and he knew he had a good product with the *Spiritual Exercises*, but he also saw that he needed help in bringing them to the broadest possible audience. This realisation motivated him to join with his roommates at the University of Paris, Peter Faber and Francis Xavier, to found the Jesuits. They encouraged others to join them in helping bring about a greater awareness of God's love. Ignatius learned he could not go it alone and that relationships with others are meaningful.

Lesson Three: Make Time for Contemplation

While recuperating from his wounds, Ignatius spent a good deal of time in bed. He had a lot of free time and was looking for entertainment. Initially, he wanted to read popular works of fiction to satisfy his active imagination. He was disappointed to find out that the books he wanted were not available, and he had to make do with holy books instead. Reading these books left him time to think about Jesus and the lives of the saints. At first, he preferred to imagine more worldly things, but progressively he found greater pleasure in daydreaming about Jesus and the lives of the saints.

By making space for something new, Ignatius began to contemplate things beyond his standard frame of reference. He began to consider the possibility that God loved him and wanted to be in a relationship with him. By opening his mind to this, Ignatius was able to make sense of things and see that he was called to a greater form of service than anything he had previously envisioned. The more Ignatius moved into contemplation, the less relevant his previous enjoyments came to be. In their place he discovered real fulfilment and contentment.